How to Become an Encore Entrepreneur:

A practical guide for those 50+ who would like to add $500 to $5,000 to their monthly income and become happier and more fulfilled in the process

By "Santa" Ed Taylor

with Jessica Vineyard

**Editing by Jessica Vineyard, Red Letter Editing,
www.RedLetterEditing.com**

More information and resources are available at:
www.Encore-Entrepreneur-Booklet.com

Contents

Introduction

In 2011 I was working as an Internet marketing coach and speaker. While I was successful at what I was doing, I was ready to do something new, something that didn't require so much ongoing research and study. I also felt a strong desire to use my skills in a way that would add more happiness to the world.

I hadn't realized it at the time, but I was about to do what millions of over-50 people are now doing: become an encore entrepreneur, or EE. This booming population comprises people 50 and older who want or need to continue working and would like their encore careers to be personally rewarding as well as bring in enough income for them to maintain a comfortable retirement lifestyle.

This book follows the stories of three people, myself included, who have navigated the transition from their former jobs to the lifestyle of an encore entrepreneur. Becoming an EE is not just about the income. At this time, in later life, it seems essential to most EEs that they also add to their personal fulfillment while increasing the happiness in their day-to-day lives. This is vastly different from getting a part-time job for economic reasons alone. Getting a part-time or even a full-time job may well be a far better solution for you.

This book will help you determine if you are a good candidate to become an EE as well as provide you with some proven tips should you determine that doing so is right for you.

We will explore whether you have what it takes to start an encore business, assess your current skills and resources, look at important resources, and discuss the first steps for you to get started on your way to being an encore entrepreneur. I will also share stories of people who are in transition and what they are doing to make a successful crossover from a j-o-b to an encore career.

Not everyone can turn a hobby or a desire into a million bucks, but many people can turn their ideas for a new career into a source of deep contentment and satisfaction while increasing their monthly income. I believe it's important that you invest as little cash as possible in a new venture while ensuring that your desired outcome is achievable. That's why I focus on stories of career changes that took minimal investment and minimal risk, yet had maximum potential to create careers that attained that desired outcome.

I hope you find these stories and guidelines helpful in deciding whether you should join the ranks of millions of baby boomers who are living longer, living better, and have never lost the desire to make a difference in the world.

~ "Santa" Ed Taylor

1: The Problem

Jessica has worked in a surprisingly wide variety of careers and had developed a number of marketable skills along the way. But after the economic crash cost her the brick-and-mortar business she had owned and run for seven years, she was at a loss as to what to do next. Her college degree in chemistry certainly wasn't any good, as she hadn't worked as a chemist in ages. And while running her business had been her full-time job for years, there wasn't exactly a market for a "luxury spa manager" after the crash. She was able to keep her house after the bankruptcy, but that was about it. For the first time in her life, at the age of 54 Jessica found herself out of a job, out of money, and nearly out of hope.

As we baby boomers swell the traditional retirement age bracket, we find ourselves far more willing and able to be senior-citizen-aged productive contributors to society than had previous generations. We want to continue working, and many of us *need* to continue working in order to maintain the lifestyle we are accustomed to. It is also true that more and more of us are finding ourselves being downsized or retired out of a job or otherwise under- or unemployed, often because of jobs lost during the recession. A lot of people are still feeling the fallout of lost retirement funds and housing investments. But the good news is that, as a consequence of the shifting tides, we are seeing the rise of a phenomenon called "encore entrepreneurs."

There are as many reasons people over fifty want or need to change careers as there are careers to choose from. I often hear about people who are getting to fifty or fifty-five and feeling unfulfilled. They still have so much to offer, and they still need an income. I have found that the over-fifty years can be a time that is deeply rewarding in terms of personal satisfaction and happiness. I also know that it is important to minimize risk while increasing the benefits of an encore career.

This book follows three people's stories on how they became encore entrepreneurs. You've met Jessica, a former day spa owner. I will share my story about how I became a professional Santa Claus, and you will also meet Jennifer, who left the pro golf world to become a pig farmer. These three very different stories illustrate the wide variety of encore careers we baby boomers are finding, livelihoods that bring us deep joy and great personal satisfaction. If you think you are a candidate for a later-life career change, keep reading, because you're sure to find inspiration in these stories as well as practical advice on how to determine if you are a good candidate for encore entrepreneurship, what your encore might be, and how to implement the tools to get you going.

I have had several careers; I had been a successful Internet marketing coach before I started pursuing my passion of bringing cheer and radiant joy to others by becoming a professional Santa Claus. People ask me what that even means, "professional Santa." We'll get to that, but in the meantime, allow me to share my story.

In 2011 I was working as an Internet marketing coach and speaker, a career I had enjoyed for several years. But I was tired of the constant research I had to do to keep up with the rapidly changing world of Internet marketing. Social media was growing faster than I could keep up with it, and I was ready for a change. I knew I wanted to do something truly fresh and new, something that would directly increase other people's joy and happiness, so I decided to turn a hobby into a stream of revenue. I had no idea how my world was about to explode.

Like many over-50s, Jennifer had done a lot of things for work. She had been in the mortgage business, which had been good for a while, but she felt no personal satisfaction. Of course, that industry eventually started going south. In the meantime, Jennifer had gotten into playing golf, so when she left the mortgage business, she took a job at a golf pro shop. Her husband was making a good salary, and they got free golf. But after four and a half years working with the pros, Jennifer knew she had to leave. She saw a side of the business she hadn't wanted to see, and it "sucked the soul out of me," she says now. "The phonies putting on airs—it just wasn't who I am. I was working weekends, odd hours, holidays, you name it. I knew I couldn't keep it up much longer."

Jennifer is not alone in feeling like her job was soul-sucking. Greater personal satisfaction and happiness are within the grasp of anyone who chooses to make them points of focus. And personal fulfillment, coupled with minimizing the risk of starting a new business, are what these stories are all about.

According to a 2011 survey by the American Association of Retired People (AARP), about half of boomers who are still working are "somewhat" satisfied with their retirement savings, but only 14 percent are completely satisfied. Also, 44 percent felt that they would not be able to do what they wanted in retirement, 36 percent may not be able to afford retirement, and 33 percent think they are probably going to struggle just to get by. This data points to plenty of motivation to continue working in some capacity as we age. Wouldn't it be nice to increase your personal satisfaction and happiness as a result of what you do for a living?

The Kauffman Foundation, an organization that focuses on education and entrepreneurship, found that Americans between the ages of 55 and 64 started nearly 25 percent of all new businesses in 2013.[1] That is a higher rate than for any other age group. The percentage of over-55ers starting new businesses has been steadily increasing since 1996 and shows no sign of slowing down soon. Another study surprisingly found that there were more founders of tech businesses over age 50 than under age 30.

---

[1] http://www.kauffman.org/what-we-do/research/2014/02/the-challenges-and-advantages-of-senior-entrepreneurship

The point is, baby boomers like you and me are redefining the retirement years. In fact, we need to come up with a new phrase, since so few of us are truly retiring. How about "the best years of our lives"? What? That's already taken?! Okay, how about "the personal fulfillment and happiness" years. It's clunky, but it will do for now.

2: The Solution

Jessica lived for a year on unemployment and her tiny savings. She took that time to look at her options. Having worked for herself most of her life, it was very difficult for her to truly consider getting a j-o-b. "I almost turned in an application to a small lab for a ten-dollar-an-hour position. Just before I clicked the 'submit' button, something in my head screamed 'STOP!' I just couldn't picture working for pittance at age 54 with no hope for advancement. I knew I had to find something that would feed me, both literally and metaphorically," she says. "As an avid lover of language and books, I had said for years that if I could be anything, I really think I'd enjoy being an editor. I didn't even know what that actually meant." Jessica says that the number one thing she tells anyone looking for a career change—or any change, for that matter—is to start by *deciding* to do it.

"Once I made the decision to become an editor, I spent most of my time researching what, exactly, editors do, what the job market is like, and how to become one," she says. She asked an acquaintance to mentor her. She talked with freelance editors she met through social media and asked them what they had done to get where they are. With the little bit of savings she had left, Jessica took that free advice and signed up for online courses to earn a copyediting certification through a prestigious university. "Yes, it was an investment—in me and my future. It took a year, but I knew I had to strengthen my basic skills and gain the technical skills I lacked."

Jessica looked for opportunities everywhere. If someone mentioned writing an article, a blog, or a book, she said she was learning to be an editor and offered to edit for free. She explains, "I didn't know what I was doing early on, but I kept thinking of the motivational education I had received from some great speakers: 'Don't wait for things to be perfect before you put it out there. Start now. Do something. Make mistakes. Just get started!' Every single day I reminded myself to be bold."

The over-50 crowd is ambitious. We are not going gently into that good night. As a generation, we are doers, we are healthier than our parents were, and we are going to live longer. We create our own opportunities. We are inventors, writers, musicians, bakers, animal lovers, and coaches. We have tools never before available to over-50s. The Internet has changed our ability to learn, research, educate, and share in ways never before possible. Combine that with our creativity and our desire to be productive, and you have a perfect mix to launch the encore entrepreneur movement.

As a former Internet marketing coach and an avid social media user, I love how the Internet has allowed us to connect online with people whom we would otherwise never meet. Entire industries have grown up around the online world, and the Internet has provided opportunities that would never have been possible without it. When I decided to turn my hobby into a revenue stream, I turned to the Internet to make the connections I needed to make my decision a reality. When I did, it was the beginning of a life change I never saw coming.

After six years of being Santa Claus as an act of community service—volunteering for community events, riding in parades, sitting for free photos with Santa, and making appearances in support of local not-for-profits—I decided to take it to the next level by taking a job as a paid Santa in a mall in Southern California.

I discovered I loved being paid to be Santa as much as I loved being a volunteer Santa. *I saw an opportunity to do something I loved and make money from it.* This is one of the many ways EEs are made: we see an opportunity, and we take action.

The next year, 2012, I decided to see if I could have an even greater impact on spreading joy and increasing happiness while making more money as Santa. I did both. In 2013 I put in more effort and saw my income and impact grow significantly. As an encore entrepreneur, I went from zero income as Santa to more than $100,000 in five years. What had started as a fun way to give back to my community became an encore career that started providing a full-time level of income the year I turned 60.

Becoming an EE holds many benefits, including the opportunity for community involvement, learning new skills, and growing in every way. Successful businesses are born from enthusiasm and passion, and many EEs experience a total sense of rejuvenation as a result of finding their long-lost passion and enthusiasm.

Jennifer became an encore entrepreneur because she saw an opportunity to live her passion and took action. "I realized I needed to quit my job, but I had no idea what I wanted to do. I had always been interested in farming and the rural lifestyle. I had volunteered for a Paleo event in 2013 and became a fan of that lifestyle, too. The two went together perfectly, Paleo and farming, growing my own food." Shortly after the event, she heard that a girlfriend had started raising pigs. Jennifer went to the farm where her friend's pigs were to see what it was all about. She ended up ordering half a pig and was impressed with the quality of the meat.

"After I got to know the owner of the farm, I approached her about being a partner," Jennifer explains. "She was very receptive, so we figured out what a partnership would look like. Before long, I had my first pig. We split everything: the work and the cost of feed, animals, and equipment. I sell my animals for profit, and most of my clients are private sales. I have sheep, pigs, and meat birds. I also have eggs, a huge garden, and a farm stand, and I source locally raised, grass-fed beef."

Jennifer goes on to say, "I had no idea what I was actually getting into. It's hard to work in the mud and the rain. Animals don't take vacations or holidays, so neither do I. It's hard to schedule down time. Feed costs are high. We work around it all because it's worth it. It has completely changed my attitude, my sense of fulfillment. I'm on a learning curve, but I'm so dedicated to learning about the animals and the whole business. It's hard to convey the full picture of what I'm doing. It's huge! Farming, gardening, watching baby pigs and lambs and chicks. I'm always entertained. The ram butts me. Princess Sparkles, the "bottle lamb," needs care. Every day is a new adventure, and I wouldn't trade it for a million bucks."

Jennifer's story shows that: 1) an interest can become a passion, 2) the passion can become a career, and 3) this can happen only when one is willing to take action. Jennifer didn't start with any animal skills, but she was willing to learn them in order to do what she loved: live a rural, Paleo lifestyle and provide others with quality food as a result.

Are you ready and able to take the leap into being an encore entrepreneur? Do you have what it takes to start a late-life business? Before you start your own business, it is essential to understand what you want to accomplish, what you are willing to do and risk, and what you *want* to do. I believe it is essential to start a business *only* if it would allow you to do something you love. In the next chapter, we will determine if you have the right stuff to launch your encore career. Let's get going!

3: Is Encore Entrepreneurship for You?

Let me say this right up front: successful encore entrepreneurs must have both enthusiasm and passion. If you don't have both, don't even start walking down the path. While I had been a professional speaker for many years, I didn't become interested in the entertainment business until I was 57 years old, and it was not something I purposely set out to do. As I wrote earlier, my new career presented itself as a result of the volunteer work I loved doing, being Santa Claus for my community. I knew before I was retained by an agent that I received deep satisfaction from the work itself. I knew I was passionate about contributing to other people's happiness. All the right components were there to help me make the transition from volunteer to professional Santa Claus, which ultimately allowed me to quit the job I had grown tired of.

Before you start your own business, it is essential to understand what you are trying to accomplish, what you are willing to do and risk, and what you *want* to do. I also believe it is important to start a business *only* if it allows you to do something you love. Strive to build a business that allows you to feel happy and fulfilled while at the same time providing a product or service that is needed or wanted.

In this chapter we will explore the question, "Do you have what it takes to become an encore entrepreneur?" I can tell you three traits and abilities right off the bat that you should have in order to be a successful EE. They are attitude, networking, and adaptability. Let's explore these one at a time:

Attitude – A successful EE has a true entrepreneurial attitude. This means that you know you will come up against obstacles, but you have a "don't quit" attitude that allows you to forge ahead (or change course, if need be). You must be dedicated and resourceful when things get tough. Having an entrepreneurial attitude means asking for help when you need it and not being too proud to do so. While many EEs are "lone wolves," they still know when to reach out for help.

Networking – This item might seem out of place in such a short list, but believe me, all successful entrepreneurs understand the importance of networking. Whether connecting through online social media, personally engaging with potential clients, or passing out your card at business events, you must be willing to step out of your comfort zone and network with all kinds of people in a multitude of ways.

Adaptability – When you can listen, understand, and apply constructive criticism and feedback, you are far more likely to build a successful business. Being adaptable also means being able to change course on short notice as a response to unforeseen events or circumstances. Very few entrepreneurial roads are paved in concrete. Most of us build the path as we travel it.

Take a few minutes to note some basic information about yourself in the questions below. After reading each one, think about the most honest answers you can give. Be as clear and descriptive as you can be. Write your responses in the space provided or on a separate piece of paper.

It is vital that you are sincerely, even painfully, truthful with yourself here. This way, you can determine not only your strong points, but also where you need to develop and increase your skills, knowledge, and character. Or, when all is said and done, you may discover that being an EE isn't for you, and that's okay. Becoming an EE can be very rewarding. But for some people, becoming an EE does nothing but add a new source of stress, frustration, and worry to their lives. Don't let your need for money or your enthusiasm about the thought of becoming an EE cloud your thinking. You know you; sit with yourself and be honest.

Encore Entrepreneur Self-Assessment Quiz

In this section, I want you to dig deep to find your honest answers, because if you don't know your own answers to these questions, you are not in a position to start a business.

Let the questions guide you to honest inquiry.

Desire

Why do you want to start an encore career? Be as specific as you can be.

What do you want to accomplish with your business?

What do you want to get out of the time you spend working?

What do you *not* want to spend time doing?

What brings you joy?

What do you do that brings others joy?

Are these actions part of your business idea? If not, how can you incorporate them?

Skills

Is your business idea based on skills you already have, or will you need to develop new ones? (It could be a combination of both.)

What will you need to do to develop the necessary skills and gain the knowledge your business idea requires?

Can you afford the skills training? Are you in an area where you can receive the training you need, or is it available online?

How long will it take to develop the skills you need?

Characteristics

While anyone can start a business, there are some basic characteristics that will improve your chances to be successful as an encore entrepreneur. Be as honest as you can here, because your answers to these questions can help you determine whether or not to move forward.

When you have failed to accomplish something in the past, how did you handle it? (Did you give up, or were you able to try another tack? Be honest!)

Running your own business takes a lot of self-motivation. Are you a self-starter? What will you do to motivate yourself when things get tough?

Do you surround yourself with people you admire and respect, or are you the one who stands out in your crowd?

A new business is a dynamic entity, and things can turn on a dime. How well do you shift with unexpected changes as they occur?

Risk

Do you know how much money you need to turn your idea into a business? Do you have that money, or can you bootstrap the business? ("Bootstrapping" means taking part or all of the money you initially make from the business and investing it right back in.)

How much money are you willing to risk?

A business can take a year or more to become lucrative. How much time are you willing to risk?

Starting and running a business means doing many things you have never done before. You must be willing to step outside your comfort zone. (That's where the growth happens!) How have you dealt with uncomfortable situations in the past? How much are you willing to stretch and be uncomfortable?

There are no right or wrong answers to these questions. The idea is simply to get you to take an honest look at what your desires, skills, and personality characteristics are. As long as you are truthful with yourself, you should be able to determine whether or not you have what it takes to be successful as an encore entrepreneur.

Now that you have made an open, honest assessment of what you bring to the table for your encore career, let's see what our three successful EEs did.

Jessica has always been an avid reader and has a natural aptitude for spelling and grammar. She knew those were the skills she wanted to use to start her business, but after doing some research into her chosen career, she realized she had few of the technical skills that successful editors need. "I really had to bite the bullet to pay for online editing classes at a top university. I had to quit going out to eat, going to movies, and spending money on extras in general. But it wasn't hard. I was truly motivated."

Jessica spent a year earning her copyediting certificate. In the meantime, she took small jobs where she could apply the skills she did have. "My confidence grew in direct proportion to the difficulty of the classes," she says. "I have always been tenacious and focused on my goals. There was just never a doubt in my mind that I would create a successful career." The majority of Jessica's investment in her encore career went into her classes. She also worked with a mentor who oversaw projects she gave to Jessica. The mentor paid Jessica a percentage from each project when it was finished. "I had to set my ego aside," Jessica admits. "I've always been a leader, so when I was in a student/mentee role, I had to constantly remind myself that I needed to learn this stuff. It sounds easy to do, but for me, it was sometimes challenging. I already wanted to be 'good enough'!"

Do you have enough money to invest in upgrading the skills or gaining the knowledge you need to launch your enterprise without affecting your long-term financial plans? It is not worth risking the money you need to get started unless you can truly afford to lose it, no matter how much you believe your business will be a success. As with any financial investment, if you can't afford to lose it, don't risk it.

Here I give two examples of potential encore entrepreneurs and how their self-assessments look. The first one is mine:

Encore Entrepreneur
Self-Assessment Quiz for Ed Taylor

Desire

Why do you want to start an encore career? Be as specific as you can be.

The money. I hope to add to my monthly income and savings for the future.

What do you want to accomplish with your business?

While money is essential, I also feel very strongly about "doing good while doing well." I want to have a positive impact on people's lives.

What do you want to get out of time you spend working?

I want to think about and share my thoughts with others who may benefit from them. I love public speaking and writing. I love bringing smiles and lifting spirits.

What do you *not* want to spend time doing?

I don't want to have a strict schedule. I don't want to persuade (but I very much want to educate and share my experiences).

What brings you joy?

I love feeling like I am contributing to the lives of others, and I love feeling that I am having a significant impact. Doing this in a big way (affecting many thousands or millions) brings me a sense of greater satisfaction.

What do you do that brings others joy?

I am friendly, interested in other people, and I make sure I understand what others desire from me. I not only provide the service I am hired to do, but I make sure that there is always added value.

How are these actions part of your business idea? If not, how can you incorporate them?

Bringing joy to others and increasing their happiness is always foremost in my mind.

Skills

Is your business idea based on skills you already have, or will you need to develop new ones? (It could be a combination of both.)

Both. I have some skills as a communicator, and as I more fully embrace the entertainment industry, I'm discovering the benefit to developing and honing new skills such as improv, dance, voice, video production, scripting, and more . . . and I love it!

What will you need to do to develop the necessary skills and gain the knowledge your business idea requires?
Mostly take classes and lessons.

Can you afford the skills training? Are you in an area where you can receive the training you need, or is it available online?
Yes, I can attend trainings.

How long will it take to develop the skills you need?
I can learn over time for as long as I need to.

Characteristics

When you have failed to accomplish something in the past, how did you handle it? (Did you give up, or were you able to try another tack? Be honest!)
I'm usually very quick at getting back on the horse . . . or finding a new horse to ride.

Running your own business takes a lot of self-motivation. Are you a self-starter? What will you do to motivate yourself when things get tough?

Yes, I work well without being directed.

Do you surround yourself with people you admire and respect, or are you the one who stands out in your crowd?

I'm more of a loner. I do have a number of business relationships with high achievers, and in some crowds I might emerge as a leader.

A new business is a dynamic entity, and things can turn on a dime. How well do you shift with unexpected changes as they occur?

I am very flexible and adjust quickly to changes.

Risk

Do you know how much money you need to turn your idea into a business? Do you have that money, or can you bootstrap the business?

I have no idea about the money required.

How much money are you willing to risk?

Less than $1,000.

A business can take a year or more to become lucrative. How much time are you willing to risk?
I am comfortable risking a lot of time, as long as I can see progress.

Starting and running a business means doing many things you have never done before. You must be willing to step outside your comfort zone. (That's where the growth happens!) How have you dealt with uncomfortable situations in the past? How much are you willing to stretch and be uncomfortable?
I am very comfortable being uncomfortable!

Now let's look deeper at my answers. One of the first things I want to point out is that I write "I don't know" when I really don't know. It's okay to not know an answer to something, as long as you are aware of it. The main idea here is that there are no right answers, but there are revealing answers. My answers reveal that I have a strong passion for having a big impact on people's happiness and contributing to society in a positive way. I am willing to work hard, I have the ability to learn new skills, and I don't want to invest much money. Even though I am a loner, I know from experience that I often emerge as a leader in group settings. This self-inquiry shows that I have what it takes to become a successful encore entrepreneur. Let's look at a self-assessment taken by someone who doesn't have the obvious characteristics typically indicative of a successful entrepreneur.

Angela Simmons is 53 and is currently employed, but she hates her job. She has always worked a 9-to-5 job. She is rather introverted, but she has always dreamed of having a dog-grooming business because she loves dogs and she likes the idea of working for herself. Angela considers herself a hard worker and follows directions well. She has always appreciated the financial security of regular employment, but she has a little savings and feels ready to explore starting her own business.

Encore Entrepreneur
Self-Assessment for Angela Simmons

Why do you want to start an encore career? Be as specific as you can be.

I want to do it because I would like to be self-sufficient and have my own hours, work when I need to work.

What do you want to accomplish with your business?

I think it would be a good service to people, and rewarding, because people would be happy with my grooming, and it would be profitable enough to make a good living.

What do you want to get out of time you spend working?

I would like to make enough money to be able to take time off to do pleasurable things, make short trips, perhaps with a goal to go someplace special and take some time to enjoy life.

What do you *not* want to spend time doing?
I don't want to waste time. Life is short; who knows how long you have to live it. I would like to be doing something I enjoy and make a living at it.

What brings you joy?
I try to spend some off time volunteering, and that gives me joy.

What do you do that brings others joy?
I think volunteering gives other people joy, too.

Are these actions part of your business idea? If not, how can you incorporate them?
Volunteering could become part of my ideas. Actually, I like that idea.

Skills

Is your business idea based on skills you already have, or will you need to develop new ones? (It could be a combination of both.)

I probably would have to develop some new ones, but I have a small amount of experience with dog grooming by having animals and doing it for friends.

What will you need to do to develop the necessary skills and gain the knowledge your business idea requires?

I would need to take some classes in how to run a business. I think I know enough about dog grooming that I don't need those classes.

Can you afford the skills training? Are you in an area where you can receive the training you need, or is it available online?

Yes, I would be able to pay for classes. I think I can take online and in-person classes.

How long will it take to develop the skills you need?

I think I can learn what I need to know in just a few weeks.

Characteristics

When you have failed to accomplish something in the past, how did you handle it? (Did you give up, or were you able to try another tack? Be honest!)

Probably most of the time I just gave up. I don't like to try things I don't think I can do.

Running your own business takes a lot of self-motivation. Are you a self-starter? What will you do to motivate yourself when things get tough?

I think I can learn to be a self-starter, but I haven't had experience in doing it much. I am willing to learn, though.

Do you surround yourself with people you admire and respect, or are you the one who stands out in your crowd?

I have friends I admire a lot. I have a friend who has her own business.

A new business is a dynamic entity, and things can turn on a dime. How well do you shift with unexpected changes as they occur?

I think I am pretty flexible, but again, I haven't had a lot of opportunity to do it in business situations. I like routine, so once the business is going well, it should feel pretty routine in the day-to-day operations.

Risk

Do you know how much money you need to turn your idea into a business? Do you have that money, or can you bootstrap the business?

I think I have an idea of how much I need. I don't think business classes cost very much.

How much money are you willing to risk?

Probably $2,000.

A business can take a year or more to become lucrative. How much time are you willing to risk?

A year would be a reasonable time.

Starting and running a business means doing many things you have never done before. You must be willing to step outside your comfort zone. (That's where the growth happens!) How have you dealt with uncomfortable situations in the past? How much are you willing to stretch and be uncomfortable?

I believe I can work hard at trying to be flexible and make changes as necessary. I think I would need to ask for a lot of help, and that could be hard for me, since I'm generally pretty shy.

Angela has a strong desire to work for herself, but she doesn't have a lot of traits that we typically associate with successful entrepreneurs. For example, she hasn't had tenacity in the past, as seen by her statement that she would just give up if she was failing at something. Her natural shyness could prevent her from seeking the advice she will surely need. We also see that she hasn't done much research in start-up costs.

While none of Angela's answers indicate that she should *not* start her business, she would do well to *learn what she doesn't know*. At this point, it seems that Angela's idea for a dog-grooming business is just an idea. Hopefully she can recognize that she would do well to overcome her fear of failure and learn to push through her innate shyness. She may decide that starting her own business is a much bigger project than she really wants to take on. Of course, she may also be sufficiently motivated to learn what she doesn't know and take the appropriate steps to get her on her way to being an EE.

It is important here that we address the idea of *who you will become*. There are three elements that I feel are very important to understand about being a successful encore entrepreneur:

1. You are doing something you feel good about.
2. Understand that having fun is a bonus, and making money makes it fun, too.
3. Consider who you will become because of your encore business.

I'm becoming a different person because of what I am learning, the people I am meeting, and the actions I am taking. I'm expanding my comfort zone. For example, I have never been a dancer, but now I'm thinking that learning to dance could help me and be fun. I am getting the impetus to learn, because more roles would become available to me.

Things that I have never pursued before, that I never dreamed of doing, are becoming more important simply by virtue of my new career. I never even thought of doing things like being a storyteller or dancer or actor. I never consciously thought of storytelling as a part of my existence just like I never viewed a movie as the "story" of the movie. Now I'm doing these things and thinking about them in a very different way. My whole focus has changed.

I feel there is a personal growth and development aspect to being an encore entrepreneur. It is important that you are open to change and are ready for growth. I find that the older we get, the more interested we are in deepening our growth as individuals and becoming closer to the person we always wanted to be, even if it looks very different from who we are now or who we have long seen ourselves to be. We *can become* who we want to be, and there has never been a better time to take the actions that will bring us happiness and fulfillment while also earning us some extra money.

4: Making the Transition

Okay, so now you have determined that you have what it takes to start your own encore business. Hopefully, you have an idea of what that business is, and you know it will fulfill your needs, wants, and desires. You know how much you are willing to invest, and you have some idea of how long you are willing to work to get the business up and running and supporting itself. You are on board with the personal growth that will almost certainly occur. You are ready to JUMP.

Now what?

In this chapter we will look at sketching a rough draft of a business plan and creating a guideline for implementing your idea. First, let's look at Jessica's process. We will use a guide that follows the scientific method:

1) Define the task (What am I trying to accomplish or know?)

2) Gather the data (What can I find out about the subject? What is already known about it?)

3) Create postulates (What do I know is already true pertaining to the task?)

4) Create a hypothesis (For example, if I do A, then B will likely happen.)

5) Test for corroboration (Did it work? This step is followed by what determining what needs to be tweaked to make the hypothesis work or work even better, then by running another test.)

Jessica had a basic idea of the business she wanted. It included the nature of the services she wanted to provide (a variety of editing services), the "mood" of her brand (friendly, positive, supportive), and what she needed to earn to cover her basic expenses. She also considered her best marketing strategy (word of mouth) and what she needed to do to upgrade her skills (offer services for free or very low cost while taking online classes). She never wrote a business plan, "but I had a vision of what I wanted," she says.

Once she decided on her type of business, Jessica did her research by reading all she could about the services she wanted to offer. "I learned that 'editing' meant much more than I thought it did. That was exciting, because the nature of the work became that much more interesting to me. I also knew that I wanted to present a warm, friendly, 'we're in this together' attitude in my branding. I emphasize that my work is not about me, it's all about my clients and their writing. I am here, above all, to be a part of their support system and to help them get their messages out exactly how they mean to." As she worked on creating her business image and developed clients, Jessica registered for the online classes. She says, "The course was a year long, so I had lots of time to make connections and lay the groundwork. I offered to edit anything I could, explaining to friends and business associates that I was still learning my skills. I really just jumped in way before I knew what I was doing. I found people to be very supportive."

Was she nervous? "Absolutely!" she says, "But I have enough confidence in my abilities to know that I could learn anything I needed to know. The hardest part was 'you don't know what you don't know.' Ignorance is my biggest enemy! I am also still determining how to bring in revenue in other ways, like holding editing workshops for writers and writing an e-book."

A lot of people never write business plans, but every business coach will tell you that you should. Interestingly, many, many EEs never write a business plan, perhaps because even the best plans cannot account for unforeseen events that can completely change the direction a business grows. In fact, the need for writing a business plan is under debate in business coaching circles. Even Forbes magazine is jumping into the fray, with an article titled "Why business plans are a waste of time."[2]

---

[2] http://www.forbes.com/sites/actiontrumpseverything/2013/08/14/why-business-plans-are-a-waste-of-time/

Do you have a business plan? If so, great! If not, the following is a very simple guideline to help you get something down on paper. It will help you see your vision a little more clearly, even if it doesn't end up being a step-by-step roadmap to your encore business.

The Not-Really-a-Business-Plan

What kind of business do I want to open? Why? (Retail, consulting, professional service, etc.)

Will my business be a sole proprietorship, an LLC, an S Corporation, a C Corporation, a non-profit, or other? What need will my business fill?

What goods and/or services will I offer? (Be specific.) What will I charge?

Who are my customers? ("Everyone" is never an answer!)

How will I market my business? (Word of mouth, print advertising, social media, etc.)

How much money do I need to open the business? Where will it come from?

Where will the money come from to keep the business operating?

Where will my business be located? (In the home, online, in a building, etc.)

What insurance will I need?

What equipment do I already own that I need for the business?

What equipment do I need to purchase or lease?

What other startup expenses do I anticipate? (Office supplies, licenses, accounting, etc.)

What experience do I have that makes me an expert?

What are my first-year goals?

Even though this is a rather general not-really-a-business-plan, it is a good way to get you to think about your business in concrete terms. You aren't expected to have a crystal ball and see the future, but you will be wise to have some idea of what you want out of your business over time. As the saying goes, if you don't know where you're going, how will you know when you get there?

When I decided to "go pro" as a Santa Claus, I did not write a business plan. I had enough entrepreneurial experience to know my answers to many of the questions above, but I figured out a lot of things along the way, since I was entering an industry I knew very little about. I have always had the attitude of "shoot-ready-aim." Just go do it. Make an offer. Identify what you want to sell. Find out who needs it, ask them to buy your stuff. It's really that straightforward.

Jennifer also did not have a business plan. "I was lucky that I got connected to a farm that was already working and had a lot in place. Shortly before I got involved, the owner of the farm had been diagnosed with Parkinson's disease and couldn't do a lot of the work that the animals require. My offer to partner with her happened at a really good time for her, too, because I was able to help with stuff she couldn't do any more. I got in there and changed things up, brought possibilities to the forefront. I came up with new business ideas, which I didn't even know I could do. I found ways to feed the animals for free using the food bank, getting expired organic raw milk products, expired grocery store food, and so on. I did all this new stuff, and my ability to see where to streamline the farm developed as my experience grew."

Jennifer did not have a lot of money to invest, but she found that working with other people in the farm venture spread out the work and the money, which has allowed the farm and her pig business to flourish.

I can't go any further without discussing values, vision, and mission. While we touched on these in the self-assessment, I want to add that one of the biggest benefits of being an encore entrepreneur is that your values are probably clear and strong at this stage in your life. Your vision of your business is not as muddied by extreme optimism, so you are less likely to make poor decisions and more likely to consider pros and cons in each decision you make. And your mission will most likely include a more altruistic and benevolent purpose than it may have in the past. In other words, you are at a time in your life where giving back or making a difference—including to yourself—is something you value, you know or can figure out how to do, and you want to include in the mission of your business.

Take Action!

It can be difficult to overcome fear and procrastination. Getting ourselves to do things, especially new things, can be challenging. You can always find reasons for postponing getting started, but becoming an encore entrepreneur happens as a result of taking action. You must DO things.

The mind can play tricks on us. You want to work on your new project because you are excited about it, but you may have some fear about doing new things such as joining a networking group or writing a sales letter or becoming active with online marketing. It's possible that you don't know the first thing to do to get started. All of these things, and many more, can result in procrastination, which often takes the form of working on what is comfortable for *way too long*.

Just find out what people want and *be the person who provides it*!

Remember, becoming an EE is about the result: adding more money, more joy, more freedom, and more personal satisfaction into your life. Becoming an encore entrepreneur is about *you*, your personal growth, expanding your comfort zone and your experiences. Adopt an "I can do this" mindset and *take action*.

5: The Practical Stuff

Okay, you have decided you have what it takes to be an encore entrepreneur and start your own business. You have a map of some kind to give you an idea of what that business will be and what it will take to get started. Now what?

I wish I could say that you start with step 1, then do step 2, then step 3, and so on. But of course, it's not like that. You may be working on several tasks simultaneously, like Jennifer did. "It's hard to remember exactly what I did, because everything felt like a whirlwind once I decided to move forward," she explains. "I bought my first pig and immediately started to learn animal husbandry by reading everything I could get my hands on. I worked with my friend in the pigpen, watching how she handled, fed, and worked with the pigs. I started to reach out to potential customers to tell them what I was doing."

Often, a single-employee business develops and evolves naturally. That's what happened with my Santa business.

Once I was retained by an agent I had to learn, mostly by trial and error, which projects to take in order to advance my career in the way that supported my wants and desires. While I knew I wanted to entertain by being Santa Claus, I had no idea what kinds of projects were available to me. For example, I never dreamed I'd land a national commercial, then another. I even took a commercial project for which I didn't play Santa Claus. It was a real stretch out of my comfort zone, as the part required some acting that certainly was not as Santa. In fact, the whole acting thing was new to me . . . and I had not foreseen "actor" as part of my career description. But the more I did it, the more personal joy I found and the more opportunities I had to spread happiness.

When I got started, I knew I wanted two kinds of customers:

1) I wanted to be hired for commercials. To accomplish this, I needed to go the normal route of having an agent who could make me aware of the opportunities available.

2) I also wanted to be hired by major corporations to be Santa Claus for their Christmas parties. To do that, I had to find out who in a company hires for that role. Where did they look for Santa's? Naturally, the answer was the Internet. I not only developed my own website, I also discovered two websites corporations use to hire Santa's. Once I figured out what I needed to do to get my new career going, *I took action*. I was able to get my listing on those two Santa websites. In a very short time, I got bookings from those listings, and now I was in business. I also found other people who were doing what I wanted to do. I got to know them, asked them questions, shared my experiences, and they shared theirs. This was a huge help, and it even resulted in bookings that I would not have otherwise received.

You will hear this over and over when you talk to successful entrepreneurs. They learn from others who are already successful at doing what they want to do. Sometimes you can simply make a few phone calls to those people. Look for patterns in the experiences and advice you hear. Ask questions about how they did it. And, of course, learning from the actual experience of others is often far more valuable than their advice might be. In other words, look at what they are doing and how they are doing it. But you must still use your brain. Don't just blindly follow; be sure the advice makes sense and is right for you. Jennifer, the pig farmer, explains, "Right away, people were suggesting that I branch into cooking and smoking hams and doing all kinds of things with the pigs. While I am learning how to smoke hams now, I wasn't at all ready for that when I first started."

How can you find out what you need to know for free? The Internet is rich with information on whatever it is you want to do. The trick is, don't spend a month figuring out what to say, and don't spend a bunch of money on a website. If your service or product is something you can market on the Internet, learn to make your own website or at least how to update the content. There are many options now that make creating or maintaining your own website so simple that anyone can do it in a day or two.

Since I can't possibly address every detail required for every kind of business people may want to have, I would like to focus here on items that every EE should consider. You will discover and learn the precise information and actions you need to take as your path unfurls before you, but that's part of the adventure now, isn't it? Here, in no particular order, are some things you may need to research:

Business structure – Your business structure can change, but think about how you want to start. Some of the most common structures are sole proprietorship, limited liability company (LLC), non-profit, and corporation. Which structure you choose will determine many things, including taxes and insurance needs.

Unless you are a sole proprietor and are going to be using your name as your business, you will want to register a business name. You do this through your state government, usually online. You can also get a tax identification number unless you want to use your social security number.

Insurance – If you go into business for yourself, you will likely want some kind of insurance. This is especially true if you have a brick-and-mortar business, a place where the public can enter or employees will access. If you already have an insurance agent (which I bet you do), he or she is a good person to start with to find out what your insurance needs will be and how to determine coverage. From trip-and-fall insurance to errors and omissions (E & O) and workers' compensation, determining your insurance needs should be at the top of your list. Be sure to learn about Business Owner Policies (BOP), even if you plan a home-based business. If you use your car primarily for business trips, a personal-coverage policy will probably not be enough. Again, check with your agent about this very important topic. Don't skimp here. I have a $2 million liability policy for my Santa performances.

Estimated taxes – There are two things you can't avoid, and you know what both of them are. Taxes are what we are concerned with here, and you will be responsible for paying taxes on any income you make. Check with an accountant to see if you should pay quarterly taxes in the first year or if you are okay waiting to determine what your first year's income will be. Take it from one who has firsthand experience with this: you do not want to fall behind on your taxes. When they are not automatically withheld from your paycheck, it can be *very* easy to do.

Licenses and permits – If you have a brick-and-mortar business, you will need a business license and probably a city license. Your local chamber of commerce can help you determine what you need to do to legally open your doors. If you sell taxable services or goods, in most states you will need a sales tax license. Many if not most home-based businesses also need licensing of some kind. For example, if you have an in-home hair salon, you will need to have the same professional license as a Main Street salon, which helps ensure you are meeting sanitation and health rules, among other things.

Degrees and certifications – Many careers require a degree or certification. Obviously you need a degree to practice medicine, but some requirements are not as obvious. For example, some states require a personal fitness trainer to be certified, and in every state you must have a degree to practice as a physical therapist. If you want to have an organic farm, the farm must be certified organic. Be sure to understand what your chosen profession requires. On the other hand, some jobs do not require certification, but you can still get one. Often this will increase not only your skill set but your credibility. Jessica has a copyediting certification, but it is not required to be an editor.

Employees – If you are going to have employees, you must understand all of the responsibilities and financial obligations that go with having them. For example, you are obligated to withhold two types of taxes from each employee paycheck, social security and Medicare, also known as FICA (Federal Insurance Contributions Act). Additionally, check with an accountant to understand paying and withholding amounts for each tax type for every employee. (For example, there are specific rules for employees who receive tips.) It can be very expensive to have employees, so be sure you factor that into your expenses.

Service/product prices – Research what pricing the current market supports for others in your type of business. If you want to have a mobile custom carwash business, see what others are charging for the same or a similar service. If the average mobile carwash price is $80, it will be hard to justify charging $150. And can you expect to get $12 for a dozen organic free-range chicken eggs if the farmer down the road is charging only $7?

Wholesale vendors – If you are starting a retail or service-based business, you will need products and supplies on a regular basis. Do your homework to find the vendors you want to do business with; don't skimp on this. Who you choose to do wholesale business with can make or break your business because you can spend a lot of money with your vendors. And price isn't the only thing to look for; you also want quality and reliability. And perhaps most importantly, you want a supplier who cares about you as a customer, who gets to know your business's needs and values. It is possible to find wholesale suppliers whose values are in alignment with yours, and you will most likely be happier with them than with the supplier whose prices are so low that they forego customer service, or even integrity, altogether. To find vendors and suppliers, ask others in your field of interest who they use. Start going to shows, events, and conferences where suppliers have booths. Your business will depend heavily on your suppliers. Choose wisely.

Business community – In my opinion, one of the best things a new business can do is join their local chamber of commerce. I have seen entire businesses built on this one action alone. Get to know the people in the chamber's office. Most chambers have weekly or bi-weekly Greeters meetings. These are meet-and-greet get-togethers that are hosted by a different business at each meeting. Typically, each business owner or representative gets a set amount of time to promote his or her business. This is an excellent way to network and get to know other business owners in your area.

All communities have fundraisers and other needs-based events. If you are starting a business that allows you to donate, find opportunities to do so. Otherwise, volunteer. Heck, do both and maximize your own sense of fulfillment and personal satisfaction while you are supporting your community. Remember, this is how I started my Santa career!

A Few Words of Caution

If you receive benefits of any kind, they may be affected by a change in your income or work status. This includes pensions, disability (SSD), social security (SSI), Medicare, and subsidized housing. It is crucial that you research and understand how your benefits will be affected should you start an encore career.

Many people are finding success with buying and reselling businesses. While much of this type of business is online through sites such as eBay and Craigslist, sometimes people meet in person to exchange cash for goods. Never go to a stranger's house alone, and never have a stranger come to your house. Meet at a public location such as a coffee shop, at least at first. Always have someone with you during a sale. While the vast majority of sales are mutually beneficial and everyone leaves happy, it is never worth taking a risk when it's easy enough to take safety measures. Use common sense and don't ever put yourself in danger.

6: Now Get Going!

This booklet just touches the surface on how to get started on your encore business, but I hope I have inspired you and given you enough information to take action. No matter how much planning you do, no matter how much research or emails or catalogs or ideas or resources or contacts or color schemes you collect, nothing is going to happen until you take action. *Take action.* TAKE ACTION! Start telling your friends and family what you are up to. Act as though your business is already happening. Because you know what? It is. It's happening the moment you decide to do it. By simply *deciding* that you are going to be an encore entrepreneur, you set in motion the most important thing that will make it happen: YOU.

Jessica never doubted for a moment that her editing career would be successful. "There was no reason for it not to," she says. "I had done my homework and found that it was a rapidly growing field. With the boom in self-publishing, all those new authors were going to need someone to edit their books. I knew the writers who had done their own homework would realize the importance of having a pair of professional eyes polish their writing. The only reason I would have failed is if I had quit trying."

Jennifer knew that, no matter what, she was going to be a pig farmer. "Once I bought that first pig, there was no going back," she says. "I was in hog heaven, so to speak, and while I had no idea what I was doing at first, I jumped in with both feet. That was the only way to do it. I already knew I had a ready-made business because I knew so many Paleo people who wanted good-quality, farm-raised meat. All I needed to do was to learn the details. Every single one of them," she laughs.

While I had no idea what my Santa business was going to become, once I decided to go for it, I had no doubt that something would happen. Santa Claus wasn't going away; he was going to keep showing up every Christmas, and I was going to be there. I was willing to work hard, to learn what I didn't know, to expand waaay outside my comfort zone to do things I never would have imagined just a few short years ago. In my late 50's, I found my encore calling, and I'm enjoying my life every single day.

If, after reading this booklet, taking the self-assessment quiz, and making a not-really-a-business-plan you feel ready to take the leap, just do it. Get started. If you haven't already, start going to chamber of commerce and business meetings. This is an easy way to get and stay inspired. Most of the time you'll find people who want you to succeed and want to support a new business. And I want to hear how you do. I want to be on your cheering team, and I want you to succeed. Because you see, that way I'll win, too. After all, we are on this planet together, and helping each other is one of the most important ways there is to spend our time, don't you agree?

Of course you do!

Thank you for reading my little book.

What do you think? Might becoming an EE be the right thing for you? If so, you can find more resources at **www.Encore-Entrepreneur-Booklet.com**.

I wish you ALL the best,

My Apologies

Sorry that this book is so short. Had I not spent so much time on it, it would be longer.

What I've included here is simple, effective and difficult.

I know that it's difficult to find your passion and often far more difficult to find a way do what you love in a way that will serve others and generate an income for you. It may well require many hours, a hundred or more, thinking. Let your mind wander, daydream, and make notes. The idea will come.

Launching an Encore business is not for everyone. Don't talk yourself out of becoming an Encore Entrepreneur but don't talk yourself into it either. Trust your gut... and ALWAYS minimize your risk.

Find more examples, videos and other useful resources at

www.Encore-Entrepreneur-Booklet.com

9 781508 668961